To. Dr. Rae Morgan.
Thank you for your support
to UBAYA.

Surabaya, 9-12-00.

Anton Prijatno
Rector.

The Mysteries of

BOROBUDUR

Text by JOHN MIKSIC
Photographs by MARCELLO
and ANITA TRANCHINI

PERIPLUS

Copyright © 1999 Periplus Editions (HK) Ltd.

Publisher: Eric M. Oey
Text: John Miksic
Illustrations: all illustrations by Lucille Tham.
Photographs: all photographs by Marcello and Anita Tranchini, except as noted: page 7, bottom, Luca Invernizzi Tettoni; page 10 courtesy of the Prentenkabinet, Leiden; page 11, top, Kal Muller; page 11, right, courtesy of the Leiden University Library; pages18-19 Luca Invernizzi Tettoni; page 22 John Miksic; page 30 Tom Ballinger.
Production: Mary Chia &Violet Wong

Distributors

Indonesia:
PT Wira Mandala Pustaka
(Java Books–Indonesia)
Jalan Kelapa Gading Kirana
Blok A14 No. 17
Jakarta 14240.

Singapore and Malaysia:
Berkeley Books Pte. Ltd.
5 Little Road #08-01, Singapore 536983.

United States:
Charles E. Tuttle Co., Inc.
RRI Box 231-5, North Clarendon
VT 05759-9700.

COVER PICTURES
Front: all photographs by Marcello and Anita Tranchini.
Back: left, from Thomas Stamford Raffles' *History of Java*, based on a sketch by H.C. Cornelius; centre, Lucille Tham; right, Marcello Tranchini.

Contents

Buddhism In Java

Buddhism enjoyed a short but intense period of popularity in central Java. All known Buddhist temples there, including Borobudur, were built within a century of one another, between AD 750 and 850.

opposite
As early as 2,000 years ago, many parts of the vast Asian continent were already linked by well-established trade routes. Buddhism spread from India to mainland and insular Southeast Asia along these land and sea routes during the first millennium AD.

below
The very first published view of Borobudur, which appeared in the second edition of the monumental work, *The History of Java*, written by Java's Lieutenant-Governor, Thomas Stamford Raffles. This view was based on a sketch by H.C. Cornelius (see page 11), it depicts large trees growing upon the monument which do not, however, obscure the main outline of the structure.

Buddhism was not in a calm, stable state during the 8th and 9th centuries when Borobudur was built. On the contrary, this was a period of intense intellectual activity. Each teacher and each country where new forms of Buddhism were developed evolved special interpretations of the religion. Indonesians must have contributed their own concepts in addition to helping spread those from India.

Buddhism was less popular than Hinduism in ancient Java. It did, however, have powerful royal patrons and both Hinduism and Buddhism were linked to two families who formed the ruling elite of Javanese society during the Borobudur period: the Sanjaya and the Sailendra.

The meaning of the word "family" in ancient Java must be explained. The Javanese have never used family names, and Javanese trace their family relationships through both males and females. Groups of kinsmen coalesce around distinguished forebears while less important ancestors are forgotten.

Buddhism in Indonesia was closely linked to an influential family known as the Sailendra or "Lords of the Mountain." This title clearly indicates that the family claimed an intimate relationship with the supernatural power which the Javanese believed hovered around mountain peaks.

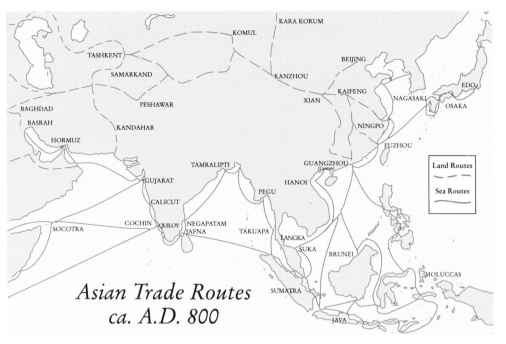

Asian Trade Routes ca. A.D. 800

Land Routes

Sea Routes

The Sailendra became the dominant political family in Java around AD 780, when they displaced the Sanjaya, an older elite who were devotees of Hinduism and had been important since at least AD 732—the date of the earliest known inscription to mention a kingdom in central Java.

Tension between members of the Sailendra and Sanjaya families must have stemmed from competition for political status, but probably had no effect on religious practices. Religion has never been a source of contention or conflict among the Javanese. The two families inter-married with the result that the children could give their loyalty to either the Sailendra or the Sanjaya.

In AD 832 the Sailendra queen, Sri Kahulunan, married a Sanjaya known as Rakai Pikatan. Pikatan gave donations to various Buddhist sanctuaries, but devoted his greatest resources and energy to the construction of the stunning Hindu complex at Prambanan.

Pikatan's reign was not entirely peaceful. Inscriptions and legends allude to war with a Sailendran prince, Balaputra, who aspired to become paramount ruler. The prince was defeated and fled to Sumatra. After about AD 850, the Sanjaya held supreme power in Java, and without the support of the Sailendra, no more great Buddhist monuments were built on the island.

Traders along the Silk Route introduced Buddhism to China during the first centuries AD, and the new religion soon acquired a firm foothold beside the indigenous Chinese beliefs of Taoism and Confucianism.

A sea link between India and China was forged around AD 400. This new route was opened by Indonesian sailors who had several centuries of experience in maritime trade with other parts of Southeast Asia and India. Buddhist pilgrims voyaged with increasing frequency through the archipelago during the 7th and 8th centuries. The records they have left tell us that Java and Sumatra were major centers of international Buddhist scholarship during this period.

Construction

It is impossible to calculate how much it cost the Javanese to build Borobudur in terms of labor and materials. Stone was plentiful and did not have to be transported far. The workmen probably used wooden carts to haul boulders from the nearby riverbed.

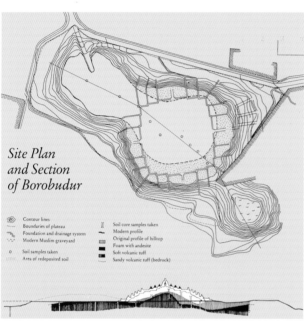

Site Plan and Section of Borobudur

Contour lines
Boundaries of plateau
Foundation and drainage system
Modern Muslim graveyard

o   Soil samples taken
Area of redeposited soil

II   Soil core samples taken
Modern profile
Original profile of hilltop
Foam with andesite
Soft volcanic tuff
Sandy volcanic tuff (bedrock)

above
Geological and archaeological studies of the ground beneath Borobudur have shown that its foundation consists of a natural hill which was reshaped by ancient Javanese builders.

hauling the stones, leveling the earth for the foundation, and terracing the hillside. The monument's stones each weigh about 100 kilograms. If one man with one cart could transport just one stone per day, it would have taken 100 men working every day about 30 years to haul one million of them up the site. Perhaps another 100 men would have been needed to load and unload the carts and hew the boulders into rectangular shapes. If, as seems likely, they worked during only half of the year, 200 men would have been required to accomplish each of these tasks.

The number of laborers needed to carve the statues and reliefs is more difficult to estimate. A modern craftsman can complete a large Buddha statue in about one month. Thus, a group of ten carvers, working at the same pace, could have completed the Buddha statues on Borobudur in about five years. Work on the reliefs was probably divided among several groups of sculptors. The masters first sketched the main outlines of the scenes, and their apprentices then did most of the rough work. The masters returned in the final stages to apply the finishing touches to the panels.

Unfortunately, the very last stage of construction is no longer visible except in minute traces. The stones we view today when we visit Borobudur were not meant to be seen at all, for the entire monument was originally coated with white plaster and then painted. The plasterwork would have required

Construction at Borobudur probably began around AD 760 and seems to have been completed by about 830. Work was probably not always kept up at the same rate during this 70-year period, but proceeded in spurts. At some times, many men must have been employed, at others only a few, and activity seems to have ceased completely during certain periods.

At least one part of the monument collapsed during its construction. Perhaps other lesser setbacks also occurred. The original plan was simpler and required less labor, but plans for Borobudur changed several times and each new design necessitated more work.

Unskilled laborers performed most of the work during the early stages:

skill, for very fine details were molded using this medium. Borobudur would then have appeared not as a dark gray mass, but as a beacon of color hovering above the uniform green of the rice fields and coconut groves.

These rough estimates suggest that Borobudur could have been built in about 30 years by a workforce of several hundred men working every day. In reality, the rhythm of work undoubtedly fluctuated seasonally to accommodate the agricultural cycle, and took 60 or more years to complete. The construction of Borobudur was a sizable task, and the achievement of the ancient Javanese is even more impressive when we consider that other temples were being built at the same time.

The majority of workers were farmers as well as part-time artisans who may have donated their labor to earn religious merit. Evidence from other temples suggests that each village contributed a group of men who formed a fixed unit within the overall labor force. Borobudur is

impressive not merely on account of its sheer size, but because it shows how large a proportion of the Javanese population had creative talents.

Religious authorities and architects probably supervised the daily activities, but the stimulus and material support must have come from the ruler himself.

top
The entrance to the eastern stairway, leading from ground level to a walkway atop the stone encasement concealing the "hidden foot" of the monument.

above
An aerial view of Borobudur from the north. Visitors on the upper terrace cluster around a stupa containing the statue known as Kakek Bima, which is credited by the Javanese with special powers.

Early Javanese Society

Borobudur tells us far more about the ancient Javanese than Javanese history can tell us about Borobudur. The monument is built of over a million blocks of stone laboriously

No traces of ancient palaces or even cities have been found in central Java, leading historians to believe that the Javanese lived in villages of approximately equal size, and that

above
A scene from the Rudrayana story in the *avadana* series on the main wall of the first gallery. This is one of Borobudur's most famous panels. The faithful minister Hiru arrives at his new home. The ship on the right is one of the best sources of information we have on ancient Indonesian ship construction. It is equipped with outriggers, like traditional Southeast Asian craft, and has several sails. The house is also realistically depicted in contrast to the rather fanciful structures found in other panels. The house's construction corresponds better to what we know of houses in other parts of Indonesia than to houses in Java. It is set on pillars and the roof employs the stressed ridge beam, like houses in North Sumatra.

hauled up a hill from a nearby riverbed, then cut and carved with great artistry. This in itself is significant, for it demonstrates that Javanese society in AD 800 produced enough surplus food and labor to support a great deal of activity which did not produce direct economic benefits. The Javanese must have had abundant manpower to haul the stones, skilled craftsmen to carve them, and well-organized institutions to coordinate such an ambitious and complex project.

Above all, it is highly significant that they chose to devote a major portion of their resources to the construction of a monument which, although it perhaps served several purposes, was principally a visual aid for teaching a gentle philosophy of life. Certainly this qualifies ancient Java as one of the most humanistic societies in history.

most of the inhabitants made their living as farmers. The fertile soil and plentiful water of the Kedu Plain surrounding Borobudur must have supported a prosperous farming population, and this may have been what attracted the monument's builders to this site. Buddhist sanctuaries usually included monasteries whose monks depended for food on contributions from the surrounding population. Archaeological evidence shows that a flourishing community of laymen, as well as clergy, lived in Borobudur's environs.

Despite their emphasis on matters of a highly metaphysical nature, the Borobudur reliefs depict many events and scenes from everyday life in a manner which seems intended to communicate with ordinary people rather than religious authorities. In between religious imagery,

Borobudur provides hundreds of examples of architecture, boats, farming practices, clothing, jewelry, dancing etc. Visitors to Borobudur probably came from all classes and might have gone there for a variety of reasons. The upper terraces provide space for meditation, but in the lower galleries people would have moved at a steady pace instead of sitting before particular panels. Large crowds could earn merit simply by walking around the monument without entering it at all.

Teachers, probably monks, would have led devotees along the galleries, explaining the tenets of the faith and illustrating their lectures with the carved panels. The journey to the summit certainly took more than a

TEN STEPS TO ENLIGHTENMENT

In order to follow the complete narrative sequence of the reliefs from beginning to end, the pilgrim had to make ten circuits of the monument—four times around the first gallery and twice around each of the next three galleries. It is probably not a coincidence that the number ten equals the number of stages in the career of a bodhisattva, one who has attained enlightenment.

single day to complete, with much time devoted to rituals. Visitors would have performed ceremonies at various stages along the way up and around the galleries. The entire process was simultaneously a physical ascent to the summit of the mountain and an intellectual ascent to the ultimate source of spiritual power.

left
Borobudur's carvers often added embellishments that had no connection with the story, including these charming animals.

Reconstruction

The first reports of Borobudur show that it was overgrown with trees and that the galleries were partially filled with dirt, but the monument was not completely buried under volcanic ash as folklore says.

Former Indonesian President Suharto officially announced the completion of the restoration project in February of 1983. Echoing the words of the famous Indonesian poet, Chairil Anwar, Suharto expressed the hope that Borobudur would now live for a thousand years more. Borobudur is now one of the best preserved ancient monuments in the world. Over a million people visit the site annually.

right
One of the earliest photographs of Borobudur, a daguerrotype by Schaefer dating from the early 1850s. The picture, of the first gallery, shows remnants of the earth which covered and protected the monument during its thousand-year slumber.

left
The 1974–1983 restoration of Borobudur was mainly funded by the Indonesian government with assistance from UNESCO and various other countries and foundations.

below
The deplorable state of the round upper terraces ca. 1908, before their restoration.

A committee was appointed in 1900 to consider measures to preserve Borobudur. One of its members was an unknown 28-year-old second lieutenant of engineers named Thadeus van Erp. When the government finally agreed to preserve the monument, Van Erp was put in charge of the project.

Van Erp began work in August 1907, and spent the first seven months excavating the plateau around the foot of the monument. He did not dismantle the monument, but tried to solve the problem of the collapsing walls and subsiding floors by covering the gallery pavement with a layer of concrete. He also rebuilt the circular terraces and their stupas. Many of the stupas had been systematically broken into and damaged by looters who dug as deep as two meters.

Van Erp did not solve the basic problem of water control. Water from the heavy seasonal rains still percolated through cracks between the stones down into the ground. The reliefs eroded further and the monument was slowly crumbling from without and within.

In 1971, a conference on Borobudur was held in central Java at the instigation of Dr. R. Soekmono, head of the Indonesian Archaeological Service. Due to his initiative and dedication, a major restoration project was conceived. The project tapped a wide range of expertise from Indonesia and abroad.

For ten years, most of the monument was closed to the public. Borobudur's principal glory—the galleries bearing the reliefs—was completely disassembled so that a complex drainage system could be installed. The project cost US$25 million, of which US$6.5 million came from foreign contributions, the rest from Indonesia's own budget.

ALMOST LOST

An excavation of Borobudur begun in 1814 by H.C. Cornelius, a Dutch engineer working under the orders of Java's Lieutenant-Govenor Thomas Stamford Raffles, continued intermittently and the last reliefs were finally uncovered in the early 1870s. Ironically, the soil which covered Borobudur, concealing its beauty, also helped to safeguard it from damage—once exposed the stones quickly began to deteriorate.

Architecture

The Javanese came to Borobudur as pilgrims—to climb this holy man-made mountain and attain spiritual merit. Buddhists could physically and spiritually pass through the ten stages of development that would transform them into enlightened bodhisattvas.

Borobudur is a monument like no other. It consists of a series of concentric terraces of decreasing size that rise like steps to a central peak. It has no roof, no vault and no chamber.

This basic simplicity of form is counterbalanced by extraordinarily rich and complex decoration. Most striking of all, perhaps, are the beautiful bas-reliefs, in all some 1,460 carved stone panels covering a total area of about 1900 square meters, with another 600 square meters of decorative carving surrounding them.

Each of Borobudur's four lower levels contains a paneled gallery. The four trace square paths around the monument, each smaller than the one below it, so when seen from above, they form four concentric boxes.

The first gallery contains four series of reliefs—two on the outer or balustrade wall (one upper and one lower), and two on the inner or main wall. To see them consecutively, the visitor must therefore walk around the first gallery four times before climbing to the next level. The second, third, and fourth galleries each have two series of reliefs, so to see them in sequence, the visitor must walk around each level twice. To see all the reliefs in their correct order, pilgrims must consequently walk around the monument ten times, covering a total distance of nearly five kilometers.

The galleries give the visitor the feeling of being in a high-walled corridor about two meters wide, with a view of the sky overhead. The galleries are not straight, but turn through four right-angle bends on each side. As pilgrims follow the reliefs, walking clockwise, with the monument always on their right, the journey is enlivened by these frequent changes of direction which prevent one from obtaining a view of the corridor extending for any great distance.

The reliefs are arranged so that as one ascends the monument the stories become more complicated and abstract. The upward physical progress of the pilgrim is thus a symbolic progress from the "world of illusion" to one of knowledge and enlightenment.

In the original design, only the third and fourth galleries had elaborate gateways topped by arches,

right
The first gallery of Borobudur. Once the pilgrim enters the corridors containing the reliefs, he is completely cut off from the outside world except for a view of the sky.

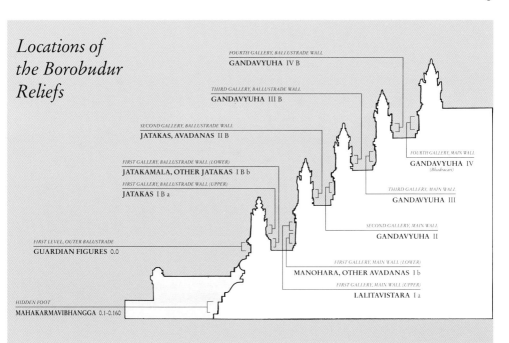

Locations of the Borobudur Reliefs

FOURTH GALLERY, BALLUSTRADE WALL
GANDAVYUHA IV B

THIRD GALLERY, BALLUSTRADE WALL
GANDAVYUHA III B

SECOND GALLERY, BALLUSTRADE WALL
JATAKAS, AVADANAS II B

FIRST GALLERY, BALLUSTRADE WALL (LOWER)
JATAKAMALA, OTHER JATAKAS I B b

FIRST GALLERY, BALLUSTRADE WALL (UPPER)
JATAKAS I B a

FIRST LEVEL, OUTER BALUSTRADE
GUARDIAN FIGURES 0.0

HIDDEN FOOT
MAHAKARMAVIBHANGGA 0.1-0.160

FOURTH GALLERY, MAIN WALL
GANDAVYUHA IV
(Bhadracari)

THIRD GALLERY, MAIN WALL
GANDAVYUHA III

SECOND GALLERY, MAIN WALL
GANDAVYUHA II

FIRST GALLERY, MAIN WALL (LOWER)
MANOHARA, OTHER AVADANAS I b

FIRST GALLERY, MAIN WALL (UPPER)
LALITAVISTARA I a

but these were later added to the first and second levels as well although most of the lower gateways have disappeared. The remaining gateways are ornate. A fearsome monster's head called a *kala* forms the top of an arch through which the visitor must pass. Ascending from the fourth gallery onto the round upper terraces, the visitor enters a very different realm. The densely packed decoration, rectilinear shapes and enclosed galleries of the lower levels are replaced by simple, curvilinear forms set on open, elevated terraces which offer distant views in every direction, imparting a liberating feeling of spaciousness.

Placed upon the three circular terraces are 72 stupas—32 on the lowest terrace, 24 on the middle, and 16 on the highest. The stupas are not solid, but consist of a stone lattice constructed in such a way that the entire surface is perforated with regular geometric openings which are diamond-shaped on the first two

terraces, but square on the third. A life-sized stone Buddha statue sits within each stupa. From outside the monument, these statues are invisible and one sees only the outer sheath.

The stupas are between 3.4 and 3.8 meters in diameter and 3.5 to 3.75 meters high. The *anda*, or body, is bell-shaped and surmounted by a square spire, or *harmika*, on the first two levels, and an octagonal one on the third. These stupas may once have contained precious objects beneath the statues, but they were ransacked by treasure hunters long ago.

At the highest point of the monument, in the very center of the structure, stands a huge stupa, measuring 16 meters in diameter and surrounded by a narrow ledge that was probably intended for placing offerings. Only fragments of the original central stupa remain.

above
Reliefs line both the main or inner wall as well as the outer or balustrade wall of each of the four galleries. The first gallery has both an upper and lower series of panels on either side, so that in all there are ten distinct series of panels. Another series of panels was originally visible along the wall of the base, but this "hidden foot" was covered during the monument's construction in order to reinforce the foundations of the building.

Symbolism

One of the chief sources of mystery and wonder surrounding Borobudur derives from the fact that its builders were able to combine such a great number of disparate elements into a harmonious whole.

Borobudur as a Mountain

At first sight, Borobudur appears to be a squat, gray mass of stone topped with many spires. This silhouette was clearly meant to suggest a mountain. The sides of the hill upon which Borobudur stands were originally terraced, so the monument is a continuation of the natural form of the hill.

Mountains were important religious symbols both in pre-Buddhist Java and also in the imagery of Mahayana ("Greater Way") Buddhism. Buddhas often chose to reveal important scriptures

first round terraces, an expansive view over the surrounding countryside is suddenly revealed, producing a unique sensation of exhilaration. This may have been intended to symbolize the bliss of ultimate Enlightenment which Buddhists believe hovers around mountain peaks.

Borobudur as a Stupa

Borobudur's summit is crowned with a large stupa surrounded by 72 smaller stupas. The stupa form originated in pre-Buddhist India as a burial tumulus of earth surmounted

right
Drawings from the second edition (1830) of Raffles' *The History of Java*, showing cross-sections of the huge central stupa. This drawing is inaccurate in several respects, for example, the central stupa contains two hollow spaces, not one.

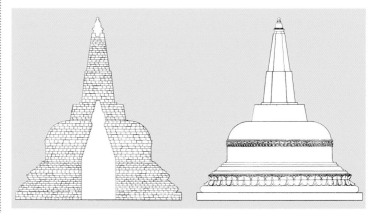

on mountain tops, while the Javanese tradition of building terraced sanctuaries on high places continues today.

Borobudur's designers intentionally created an extraordinary physical effect. As one walks through the enclosed galleries containing the reliefs, one gradually forgets about the outside world. But as the pilgrim emerges from the galleries on to the

by a wooden pillar symbolizing the link between heaven, earth, and the underworld. Stupas can either be burial markers or containers of precious relics. When Borobudur was first described in detail, the central stupa had a large hole in it revealing two empty chambers inside, one above the other, but no relics were found.

left
A Vajradhatu or "Diamond World" mandala, based on a 9th-century Tibetan version. Double circles indicate the location of 37 main deities inside the square and 1,000 deities outside it. Four *vajra* (thunderbolt) motifs decorate the outer circle at the four cardinal points.

below
A view of Borobudur from the northwest corner.

THE MANDALA

Mandalas are used in ceremonies to initiate people into higher levels of spiritual power. Mandala means "circle," but in Buddhism the word came to mean a diagram with pictures or statues of gods in specific positions. Mandalas can be painted on flat surfaces or drawn on the ground with colored powder, though in their original form they may have been three-dimensional structures.

Borobudur as a Mandala

Borobudur's design is similar in many respects to a mandala. The statuary in the niches on the balustrades which face the four compass directions correspond to the four Buddhas who surround the Supreme Buddha. The outside of the lowest balustrade illustrates a panoply of guardian figures similar to that represented in the Dharmadhatu or "Matrix World" mandala. So many details of Borobudur's construction are consistent with mandala concepts that we may be sure that Borobudur served many of the same functions as a mandala. It was a space from which evil forces had been excluded, where gods could be invited to descend and take up residence, and probably where initiates could be inducted into higher states of consciousness.

Bhumisparsa mudra

Vara mudra

Dhyana mudra

above and opposite
The six *mudra* positions
displayed by 504 life-size
Buddha statues.

Statues

Many scholars believe that the 432 Buddha statues on the five balustrades of the lower levels are linked to the 72 statues on the upper round terraces as part of a single metaphor.

The statues on the lower four levels—92 on each side—depict Buddhas with *mudras* corresponding to those mentioned in many Buddhist texts. The statues on the east side lay their right hands across their knees, palm down, in the sign of the *bhumisparsa mudra* or "seal of touching the earth." This represents Gautama Buddha (see page 26) and his battle against the demon Mara when he called upon the Earth Goddess to testify to his many sacrifices. The statues along the south side are depicted with a *vara mudra*, the right hand held palm up, symbolizing charity. Those on the west display meditation, *dhyana mudra*, with both hands on the lap, palms up, while the statues facing north hold their right hands up, palms facing out, in *abhaya mudra*, eliminating fear. On all four sides of the top row are 64 other statues in a fifth hand position, *vitarka mudra*, the right hands held up, thumb and forefinger touching, signifying preaching.

The three rows of stupas on the circular terraces around the central stupa contain a sixth type of Buddha with the *mudra* symbolic of the preaching of the first sermon, called "turning the wheel of the doctrine." This symbolizes that Buddha's sermon set the process of salvation in motion. Mahayana Buddhists believe that Buddha first preached this sermon on the summit of Mt. Sumeru, which provides additional evidence to support the theory that Borobudur represents this sacred mountain.

The depiction of six instead of five types of Buddhas has posed a problem for scholars. Most scriptures list only four perfected Buddhas, each identified by the direction they face and their *mudra*. The Buddhas on the lower niches of Borobudur face in the correct directions and have the proper *mudras* of the four

KAKEK BIMA

Historically speaking, the most popular statue, Kakek ("Grandfather") Bima, can be found to the right of the stairway on the east side of the first terrace. Kakek Bima was the second of the Pandava brothers in the Hindu *Ramayana* epic. Childless women in particular stretched out their fingers towards him in an attempt to touch him as he sat motionless in his "cage," or sometimes spent the night in a gallery or on the terrace near him, believing that by doing so they had gratified Kakek Bima.

Abhaya mudra

Vitarka mudra

Dharmacakra mudra

The central stupa may represent Buddha in Nirvana and also in his bodily form, when he is known by Mahayana Buddhists as Sakyamuni. The upper round terraces have no balustrades, unlike those below and may be a quite literal rendition of the "open space" created by Buddha for the myriads of deities who are emanations of himself. The round terraces may therefore represent the earth temporarily transformed into a paradise where the Buddhas have assembled. The statues on the round terraces face outward rather than toward the central stupa, suggesting that they are preaching the scripture to us.

The Buddha statues in perforated stupas may symbolize the Buddhist instruction that a stupa only visible to beings already "awakened" should be built wherever the scripture is preached.

perfected Buddhas: Aksobhya (east), Ratnasambhava (south), Amitabha (west), and Amoghapasa (north). Vairocana is often illustrated with the *mudra* "turning the wheel of the law," like the Buddhas in the perforated stupas on the round terraces.

The problematic Buddha is the one displaying the *vitarka mudra* on the fifth level of the monument. Some have speculated that this Buddha also represents Vairocana, but scholars disagree whether Vairocana was depicted with such a *mudra* at this period.

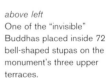

above left
One of the "invisible" Buddhas placed inside 72 bell-shaped stupas on the monument's three upper terraces.

left
A Buddha figure in the *dharmacakra mudra* pose, representing the "turning of the wheel of the doctrine"— one of the 72 identical images on the three upper terraces.

following pages
An aerial view of Borobudur seen from the north.

Visual Vocabulary

Borobudur's carvings display a wide range of motifs with symbolic meanings. Even if we do not understand specific stories in the reliefs, we can still identify the main characters depicted by referring to the symbols found in them.

The motifs used on Borobudur are also found on central Javanese Hindu temples. The two religions shared a standard artistic vocabulary, much of which came from India.

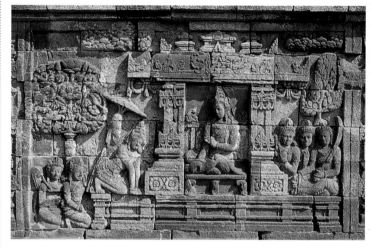

above
A *kala* head overlooking the passageways.

above right
Sudhana visits a Night Goddess to announce that someone has just attained enlightenment. Sudhana, on the left, assumes his characteristic position when visiting "Good friends," kneeling with both hands on the floor. He is shaded by a parasol.

Fly Whisks These were associated with royalty and took the form of pointed tufts of hair, either attached to the tips of parasols, or carried alone, usually by women who stand on either side of the noble person whom they serve.

Jewel Trees In the course of many travels, Sudhana, hero of the *Gandavyuha* stories (page 28), saw "jewel trees called 'treasury of radiance,' which looked like incomparable jewels and bore riches in buds producing garlands and ornaments of celestial jewels and wish-fulfilling gems, and were adorned by jewels of countless colors."

***Kala* Heads** According to one Hindu legend, Kala was created by Siva to kill a titan, while in another legend, the head represents a demon called Rahu. Gods and demons once churned the ocean to make an elixir of immortality. Rahu stole some of it.

A god cut off his head, striking him in the mouth with a sword, but because he had already swallowed the liquid, he did not die. Thus Kala's head normally is depicted without a lower jaw. Kala symbolizes the elixir of immortality, which is shown by strings of jewels or other ornaments hanging from the monster's upper jaw.

Kinnara These are mythical celestial beings, normally with the legs and wings of birds and the torsos and heads of humans. They are associated with music, which they are said to play for the gods on Mt. Sumeru.

Lotuses The lotus is found in almost every Buddhist work of art. It often serves as a throne for Buddhas and a base for stupas, while bodhisattvas carry a long-stemmed lotus in one hand.

Naga This Sanskrit word literally means "snake" but in Java it

normally refers to serpent deities. Serpents in ancient Java and India were usually connected with water and fertility. They can be either good or evil. On Borobudur, they are depicted in human form, but elsewhere they may appear in their natural animal shape.

Makaras This mythical beast with an elephant's trunk, parrot's beak and fish's tail appears very often as an artistic motif in both Hindu and Buddhist temples. A water symbol, *makaras* can also symbolize the energy excited by desire. They are found on either side at the bottom of the stairs on almost all Javanese temples, sometimes with lions, parrots, warriors, or garlands in their open beak. They are also found at either side of the doorways leading to Borobudur's different levels.

Parasols These were very important symbols of royalty in ancient and recent times, both in India and Southeast Asia. The color and number of tiers of each parasol reflected the rank of its owner. Parasols occur frequently in the reliefs on Borobudur suggesting that a similar custom existed in eighth-century Java. Many stupas, including the main stupa of Borobudur were topped by multi-tiered stone parasols symbolizing Sakyamuni's royal birth.

top
In a scene from an unidentified story, a king (or bodhisattva?) holds a lotus stem while seated on a throne supported by a lion.

above
A dancer carrying a fly whisk.

far left
A celestial jewel tree.

left
A *makara* head with a lion in its mouth flanking one of the main stairways.

Mahakarmavibhangga

Before the broad foot was added to Borobudur, a series of reliefs were visible from outside the monument. These were located just above the ground and served as moral lessons to pilgrims.

right
This panel contrasts the serene life of a temperate family on the right with the unseemly behavior of dancers, drinkers and molesters on the left.

opposite below
A number of people treating a man who is ill. They massage him and bring him ointments and medicine.

The reliefs at the foot of Borobudur depicted men and women performing both good and evil deeds and then being rewarded in heaven or punished in hell for their actions.

Mahayana Buddhism possesses several texts which describe at length the effects of specific actions. The text which the designers of Borobudur illustrated in these reliefs was a version of a Sanskrit work known as the *Mahakarmavibhangga*, or "Great Classification of Actions." None of the extant versions, however, is exactly the same as that illustrated on Borobudur. In fact, the Borobudur depictions vary more from known textual versions than any other reliefs on the monument.

The *Mahakarmavibhangga* reliefs encompass more than 160 panels, each measuring about two meters wide and 67 centimeters high. They were discovered by accident in 1885, and a complete photographic record was made in 1890–91.

Thereafter, they were covered up again and have not been seen since, with the exception of four panels that were left uncovered in the early 1940s at the southeastern corner of the monument and may still be seen there today. The panels follow a standard format—they first depict an action, then show its reward or punishment.

THE INSCRIPTIONS

It seems that originally all the panels in this series had short inscriptions above them but most were chipped off.
They may have been meant as directions to the sculptors.
They were usually single words such as "heaven," "bell," "village chief," or "king."

The hidden reliefs depict various hells and heavens from Buddhist mythology. There are eight hot hells. In one relief, men are shown fighting, and in the next panel, they are shown atoning for their sin in the Sanjiva hell, where they tear at each other with bare hands that have iron

nails, while a bird with a metal beak attacks them. The murder of innocents is repaid in Raurava hell, where the criminals are impaled on the metallic thorns of huge trees.

There is a system of sub-hells also, where sinners walk on grass-like spears or through burning water, or are trampled by elephants for various misdeeds.

The depictions of the different heavens are not nearly so elaborate. These are nearly identical and each representation has emblems of wishing trees and a pair of *kinnaras*, birds with human heads.

These reliefs were intended to prepare the pilgrim to ascend the monument by acquainting him with the difference between good and evil, and reminding him of the desirability of escaping from the sorrow of existence by achieving Nirvana. However, even before the monument was finished, these reliefs were buried.

The new foot covering the *Mahakarmavibhangga* reliefs provided a broad processional path along which pilgrims could walk to perform the meritorious *pradaksina*, or ceremonial circumambulation, around the stupa. This path had a low surrounding wall which has since disappeared.

While walking along this path, visitors can inspect portraits of various magical beings—guardian monsters, forest nymphs, and *nagas*, or water spirits, associated with rivers and lakes. Also shown are men flanked by women holding musical instruments, jewels, flowers, and fans. These do not symbolize any particular mythical beings, but were perhaps merely intended to reinforce the idea that when one enters the first gallery, one begins to ascend the holy mountain and enters a realm populated by supernatural beings and forces.

Jatakas and Avadanas

Borobudur illustrates quite a number of *jataka* and *avadana* stories in just a few panels. The stories can be compared to animal fables, fairy tales, romances, and adventure stories. Some *avadanas* have very little religious significance.

Jataka, or "Birth Story," narratives depicting acts of self-sacrifice performed by Buddha in his earlier incarnations, and *avadanas*, or "Heroic Deeds"—similar stories which differ from *jatakas* only in that the main character is not Buddha in an earlier incarnation—fill 500 panels on the balustrade of the first gallery and 120 panels on the main wall (beneath the *Lalitavistara*, see following pages), and another 100 panels on the balustrade of the second gallery, a total of 720 panels.

The *Jatakamala* Birth Stories
The stories essentially promote the notion of self-sacrifice. Numbers in parentheses refer to the lower series of relief panels on the first balustrade (IB.b), numbered consecutively from the east stairway and proceeding clockwise. The first eight stories are:
Story 1 (panels 1–4): The future Buddha becomes a hermit in the mountains and meets a starving tigress, to whom he gives his body as food.
Story 2 (5–9): The future Buddha is a king. The god Indra comes in disguise as a blind man and Buddha gives him his eyes.
Story 3 (10–14): A man and woman who give food to monks are reborn as a king and queen.
Story 4 (15–18): The future Buddha

right
A scene from Story 8 in the *Jatakamala* series: the future Buddha, on horseback, is attacked by a band of ogres, but is unharmed.

below
A scene from Story 6: the future Buddha as a rabbit. When Indra (left) arrives disguised as a Brahman, the rabbit's three friends—a jackal, an otter and an ape—all bring food. He is unable to do so, and instead jumps into the fire himself.

opposite
The merchant Maitrakanyaka greeted by 16 nymphs (here represented by 11). Each time he moves to a new city, more *apsaras* (supernatural female beings) come out to greet him.

as head of a merchant guild. He and his wife take food to a monk although to do so they have to pass over hell.

Story 5 (19–22): Reborn as a rich and highly charitable man, the future Buddha is tested by Indra, who steals his possessions. The future Buddha becomes a humble grasscutter, but retains his generous nature and is rewarded.

Story 6 (23–25): The future Buddha is a rabbit who teaches his friends—a jackal, an otter and an ape—the importance of generosity. When Indra appears disguised as a Brahman, his friends all bring food, but the rabbit is unable to do so and jumps into the cooking fire himself.

Story 7 (26–28): The future Buddha is a rich man, but becomes a hermit. As a reward for his charity to a Brahman—Indra in disguise—he is granted his wish: food of the gods in order to feed the poor.

Story 8 (29–35): The future Buddha is born as a generous king named Maitribala. Forest ogres come to the

kingdom but are unable to cause harm. The ogres ask the king for a human to eat. He has himself cut up and they are so struck, they mend their ways.

The *Avadanas* Heroic Deeds

Three of the identified stories are:
The Prince and the Nymph Manohara (panels I.b1–20): The first narrative tells the story of Prince Sudhana and is found in the lower series on the main wall of the first gallery, beneath the Life of Buddha reliefs.

Mandhatar, the Prince Whom Pride Nearly Destroyed (I.b31–50): Although this story has been identified as the inspiration for this series of panels, the reliefs deviate significantly from extant textual versions. The panels appear on the main wall of the first gallery in the lower series.

Indra and the Virtuous Sibi King (I.b56–57): Indra, king of the gods, subjects virtuous men to various trials.

Unfortunately, only a small proportion of other panels in the *jataka-avadana* series have been deciphered and the majority remain "unreadable." Several ancient compilations of *jatakas* contained a total of 100 separate tales, and there is some indication that the Borobudur reliefs depict approximately that many stories too.

The order of stories on Borobudur after the first 34 does not correspond to any known collection. It is possible that Borobudur's builders did not refer only to a single source, but combined the *Jatakamala* with individual stories selected from a variety of sources. Perhaps some were never written down, but were passed on orally.

The *Lalitavistara*

Reliefs depicting the life of Buddha cover the upper half of the main wall all around the first gallery of the monument, a total of 120 panels. These reliefs were carved to illustrate a text entitled the *Lalitavistara*, "The Unfolding of the Play."

All approaches to Borobudur look the same. Only when scholars began to identify the narrative reliefs did they discover that the main entrance lay to the east, because the stories begin there and proceed clockwise around the galleries. This suggests that visitors were meant to approach Borobudur from this direction.

Those entering the monument climb the eastern stairway to the first gallery and turn left to begin their journey, so that the monument is always to their right. To view the relief panels in sequence, visitors walk clockwise around the monument, performing a ceremonial circumambulation which earns spiritual merit.

Visitors to the first gallery see four series of reliefs—two on either side of the gallery, an upper and a lower one. Three of these are devoted to the *jataka* and *avadana* tales. The most prominent set of panels, however—the upper series—illustrates the life of the historical Buddha, Sakyamuni or Siddharta Gautama.

The *Lalitavistara* refers to the idea that Buddha's last incarnation was a performance intentionally given to enlighten mankind before he vanished from existence. The reliefs of Borobudur are the most elaborate depiction of this drama on any monument in the world.

Gautama was not a real person, but an identity assumed by a bodhisattva in order to fulfill his duty to help other beings attain liberation. Borobudur was not a monument for the worship of Gautama, but an instrument to teach people how to become bodhisattvas, as well as a place where they could be assisted to achieve that goal. Gautama was only one example, although a primary one, of how others had attained Nirvana.

As a group, the panels on the first gallery are among the best-preserved on the monument, except for some on the south wall. The protective

blanket of soil which the centuries laid over parts of the monument was probably deepest in the first gallery.

"The Unfolding of the Play"
Episode 1: The Prelude to the Birth of Buddha: Panels 1–15, leading from the eastern stairway of the first gallery to the southeast corner. The panels begin by describing the future Buddha in the Heaven of Contentment, one of the levels of paradise in Mahayana Buddhism.

Episode 2: The Birth and Early Life of Buddha: Panels 16–45, on the southern side. Queen Maya gives birth to Sakyamuni in the Lumbini Pleasure Garden, illustrated in panel 28.

Episode 3: Buddha's Marriage and Renunciation of His Earlier Life: Panels 46–75, on the western side. Describes the Four Encounters which motivate the prince to undertake his quest for enlightenment.

Episode 4: Buddha's Enlightenment: Panels 76–105, on the northern side. Sakyamuni attains Supreme Enlightenment and becomes Buddha, the "Enlightened One" in panel 96.

Episode 5: The Preaching of the First Sermon: Panels 106–120, on the eastern side to the north of the stairway. The narrative ends as Buddha preaches the fist sermon, which sets the "Wheel of the Law" in motion, at the corner of the eastern staircase.

Queen Maya's procession. The queen is shown escorted by members of the Sakya tribe. The sculptors mark the movement of people by tilting the parasols and standards (panel 27).

Sakyamuni has left the palace and dismissed his horse and groom. Sakyamuni stands at the left beneath a parasol, bidding farewell to the supernatural beings who accompanied him (panel 66).

Sakyamuni bathes in the Nairanjana River, attended by gods who sprinkle him with perfume and flowers. On the right bank, two naga water spirits raise their heads from the river (panel 86).

Sakyamuni subdues the demon Mara. The Earth Goddess arises with a vase in her hand just beside the prince's right hand. Mara is on the elephant just in front her (panel 94).

The *Gandavyuha*

Of all the stories told on Borobudur, the most space is devoted to a tale about a youth named Sudhana and his quest for wisdom. The three highest galleries are reserved for this story about a boy who travels far and visits many teachers.

Sudhana's story is told in 460 panels. It begins on the main wall of the second gallery (128 panels), continues on the main wall of the third gallery (88 panels), fills the balustrade of the fourth gallery (84 panels), and then reaches its conclusion on the main wall of the fourth gallery (72 panels).

The literary work which the artists illustrated is entitled the *Gandavyuha*, "the Structure of the World Compared to a Bubble." There are no adventures or romances, just repetitive visits to various teachers, alternating with mystical visions experienced by Sudhana and others.

The *Gandavyuha* begins with Buddha and the bodhisattva Samantabhadra (the "Universally Good") in a garden with the Buddha Manjusri and virtuous human kings, surrounded by 5,000 bodhisattvas. They ask Buddha to perform a miracle for them, which he does by going into a meditation called "the appearance of the lion," which causes beautiful visions to appear. Most of the scripture is a repetitive account of Sudhana's long journey to visit spiritual instructors ("Good Friends"), each of whom imparts wisdom to him before sending him on to the next guru. Sudhana eventually reaches the palace of Maitreya, the next Buddha.

Sudhana's pilgrimages are allotted only 126 of the panels, while the remaining 334 panels depict scenes and events which take place after Sudhana's arrival at Maitreya's palace, as well as his meetings with two other supernatural teachers: the Buddha Manjusri (panel IVB.51) and the bodhisattva Samantabhadra (panel IVB.70 or 71). It is Samantabhadra who has the honor of imparting the highest wisdom to Sudhana. The climax of the entire series of 1,460 reliefs on Borobudur comes when Sudhana vows to follow the example of Samantabhadra.

The lesson which the scripture implies is that one should not expect to find enlightenment only in one place, or from one source. Sudhana's Good Friends are women, men, and

children from all levels of society, as well as supernatural beings. Anyone is eligible for enlightenment and there is no suggestion that wisdom is something to be jealously hoarded and imparted only to the elite.

The scripture frequently makes the point, however, that different people have varying capacities for understanding Buddhist teachings, and that the lessons have to be adapted to the level of the student. Thus, Borobudur does not seem to have been meant only for learned religious students, but was also for those visitors who reached this level of the monument. They would have needed to have an open mind in order to benefit from the instructions of the reliefs on the upper galleries.

On the east face, the reliefs conclude with the final passage from the Gandavyuha in which Buddha himself tells Sudhana that all

bodhisattvas, monks, and the great disciples are elated and applaud the vow which he and Samantabhadra have made (IV.72). No doubt pilgrims who reached this stage of instruction now identified themselves with Sudhana and felt that by their perseverance, they too had given all the Buddhas cause for joy.

above
A scene from one of Maitreya's past lives, as a ruler in a palace. Mythical half-human birds (*kinnaras*) fly above the pavilion. Dancers and musicians are depicted in a scene that was undoubtedly familiar to Borobudur's artists (panel III.65).

below
The bodhisattva Vimaladhvaja in meditation (panel II.113).

The Message

Borobudur's main meaning is most likely to be found in the complex relationship that exists between the reliefs and the architecture. In order to understand Borobudur, we need to solve the riddle of the monument's structure.

right
A Buddha image on the upper terrace at dusk. Night was an auspicious time according to Buddhist belief, when many beings attained enlightenment. Monks probably meditated on the round terraces by starlight.

opposite
top view of Borobudur. The mandala-like pattern of the monument is evident when seen from this perspective. Borobudur has also frequently been compared to a lotus, and the three concentric rings of stupas are indeed reminiscent of the seed pods at the heart of the lotus flower.

Borobudur expresses a complex message in a code that has yet to be cracked, partly because the range of individual elements making up the code is so vast. Why are there six square terraces and four round ones? Why do the niches on the bottom balustrade have a jewel motif, while those on the upper four balustrades have a stupa motif? Why are the 72 perforated stupas at the top divided into two types: one with diamond-shaped holes and square bases on the two lower terraces, another with square holes and octagonal bases on the upper terrace?

Scholars have devoted a great deal of energy to the search for a single concept which would explain every aspect of Borobudur's design. According to one theory, the round upper terraces were meant to form the base for an enormous stone stupa which contained a precious relic of Gautama Buddha. Some have said that a stupa is indeed all that Borobudur is. Another theory proposes that Borobudur has a tripartite structure representing the three Buddhist realms of existence: Desire, Form, and Formlessness. Another theory speculates that it was designed as a giant mandala or a sacred enclosure for use in initiation rites. Yet another theory asserts that the monument was above all a symbol of the royal might of the Sailendra rulers. Finally, for some,

NEW METHODS

At the time Borobudur was being built, Buddhism was in transition and Buddhists believed their faith was developing new and more effective methods to achieve spiritual liberation. People were experimenting with special ritual practices, diagrams and other physical aids to help them attain enlightenment.

Borobudur represents the abode of the gods, sacred Mt. Sumeru, situated at the center of the cosmos.

Borobudur's design cannot be reduced to a single element; rather it combines three principal motifs: mountain, stupa, and mandala. Although each element had unique connotations, their symbolism overlapped. Borobudur's designers succeeded brilliantly in linking the three to create an integrated, coherent monument.

It would be far too simplistic, therefore, to expect to discover one fundamental idea to account for all aspects of Borobudur's complex form. The monument has multiple layers of meaning which accumulated during its active life, and it therefore represents a process of cultural evolution rather than a single moment in Javanese history. One of the chief sources of mystery and wonder surrounding the monument derives from the fact that its builders were able to combine such a great number of disparate elements into a harmonious whole.

Borobudur is the only surviving monument of its type in Java. Other Buddhist structures have rooms and were designed to house icons. Borobudur's design is so different from these structures that it seems logical to conclude that its purpose also differed. It was not intended as a place to show devotion to the Buddhas, but rather as a place to achieve the practical end of becoming a bodhisattva.

Top View of Borobudur

0 1 2 3 4 5m

GLOSSARY

Bodhisattva

Someone who has attained Enlightenment but chooses to postpone his ascent to Nirvana (see Enlightenment) in order to help others find Enlightenment. Some Buddhists revere particular bodhisattvas and representations of bodhisattvas can be found in temple sculptures, wall paintings and scriptures.

Brahman

The name given to someone who is a member of the highest or priestly class of Hindus.

Enlightenment

The name given to the highest state of religious awareness that can be accomplished by a Buddhist. The achievement of Enlightenment requires the attainment of spiritual awareness and intellectual knowledge. Once a follower of Buddhism has found Enlightenment then he may ascend to Nirvana, a heavenly state which frees the individual from the pain and suffering of the cycle of reincarnation.

Indra

The Hindu god of rain and thunder and the chief of the Vedic gods.

Mahayana Buddhism

Originating in South India at the beginning of the Common Era, followers of Mahayana Buddhism called their view of the spiritual teachings of Buddha the 'Great Vehicle', they called everything that had gone before the 'Lesser Vehicle'. Mahayana Buddhism took a more altruistic view of the individual's involvement in Buddhism, for example, where mainstream Buddhism applauds the individual's search for Enlightenment and Nirvana, Mahayana Buddhism applauds the bodhisattva's willing postponement of Nirvana due to his desire to help others achieve Enlightenment.

Mudra positions

Ritual hand positions which signify symbolic meanings.

Raffles, Thomas Stamford

(1781-1826) English colonial administrator of Java, founder of modern-day Singapore

Ramayana

An epic series of Indian stories about the adventures of Ramachandra and his wife, Sita.

Sakyamuni

The name given by Mahayana Buddhists to Buddha in his bodily form.

Stupa

Originally, a monumental pile of earth or rocks erected in memory of Buddha, or as a marker on a sacred spot. Stupas gradually became more and more sophisticated, eventually evolving into structures that required architectural expertise to contruct.